This book is dedicated to my family, and especially my grandbabies, and to all the other "tator" tots and "princess fluffy toes" that I love so much!

© 2022 Kerry E. Garner, Publisher of Record
Tulsa, OK 74133, Instagram Kerryegarner
All RIGHTS RESERVED
No Reproduction of this work in part or
in whole is given without consent
The people and situations in this book may
be inspired by people in real life, but in no way
claim to represent said person's
true thoughts, feelings, words, or actions.

The Wholesome Promise only reflects
the Author's view as to what she considers
wholesome.

ISBN #:979-8-9863470-2-8 paperback
ISBN # 979-8-9863470-3-5 e-book
LCCN #2022910441
Edition #1
Book 2 of "WITH THE ANIMALS AND ME" Series

Kerry E. Garner

ABOUT THE AUTHOR

Kerry E. Garner is an author dedicated to her faith, family, community, and country. Growing up in the beautiful South Arkansas town of Hamburg, Kerry was provided a fertile ground that enriched and nurtured her love of God. She graduated from Oral Roberts University with a degree in English Literature. She married the love of her life, Frank Garner, in 1990, and they raised two incredible sons. Kerry founded a faith-based women's Bible study in 2000, a steadfast endeavor through which she continues to impart the teachings of God to this day. Over the course of two decades, Kerry served her church, offering comfort, encouragement, and a prayer of faith for those in the hospital and those needing altar ministry, where she also served as team lead. Today, she dedicates herself to her family, Ladies' ministry & healing ministry. Attends daily morning prayer at Rhema Bible College and serves as an altar counselor at Victory Church in Tulsa, OK. She continues to study God's Word and looks forward to writing more books. Kerry is available for women's ministry speaking engagements and can be contacted at 918-971-8440 or Kerryegarner@gmail.com.

Testimonials of breakthrough can be sent to the same email address or sent on messenger to Kerryelisabethgarner on Instagram.

Books by this author can be found on Amazon.com under Kerry E. Garner Books:

A Prayer Warrior's Weapons of War: Rescuing the Lost, Stalked & Prodigals

Children's Book:

The Adventure Series:

Brandon and Brad's Backyard Adventure
Brandon and Brad's Water Park Adventure
Brandon and Brad's Pirate Ship Adventure
Brandon and Brad's Grandparent Adventure
Brandon and Brad's Italian Family's Adventure in Buffalo, NY

With the Animals and Me Series:

Come ABC with the Animals and Me
Come 123 with the Animals and Me
Princess Fluffy Toes Loves to Dance
When Jenny Met Jesus: A Prayer of Salvation for Children
Psalms 23 for Children: Empowered to Face Fears, Bullies, and Life in the Real World

Come 1 2 3

WITH THE ANIMALS AND ME

Written and Illustrated by
Kerry E. Garner

1

One little elephant,
eating a pie.

2

Two tall giraffes, jumping so high.

3

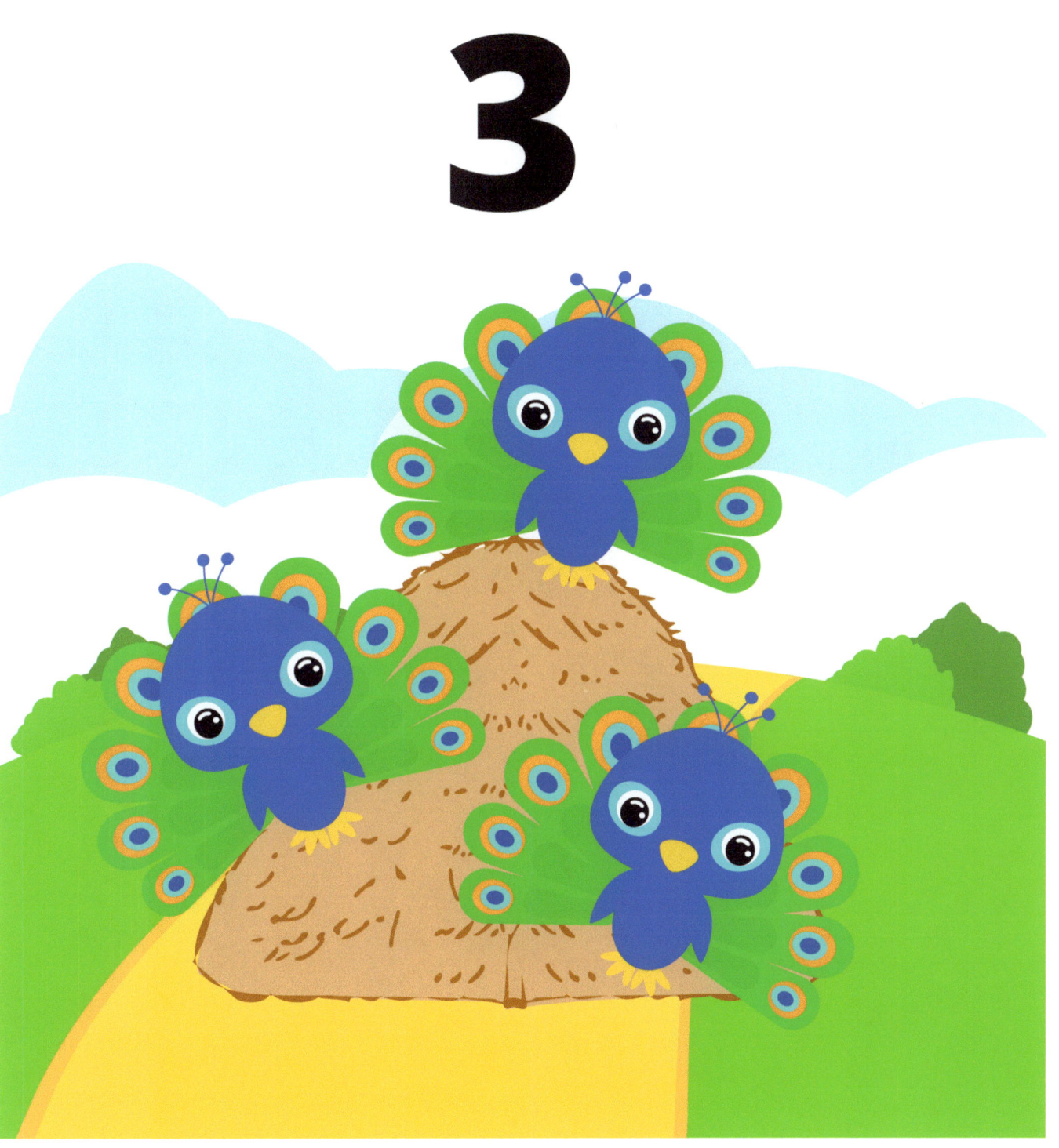

Three little peacocks, climbing on hay.

Four brown cows, enjoying the day.

5

Five baby whales,
exploring the sea.

6

Six monkeys playing, high in the tree.

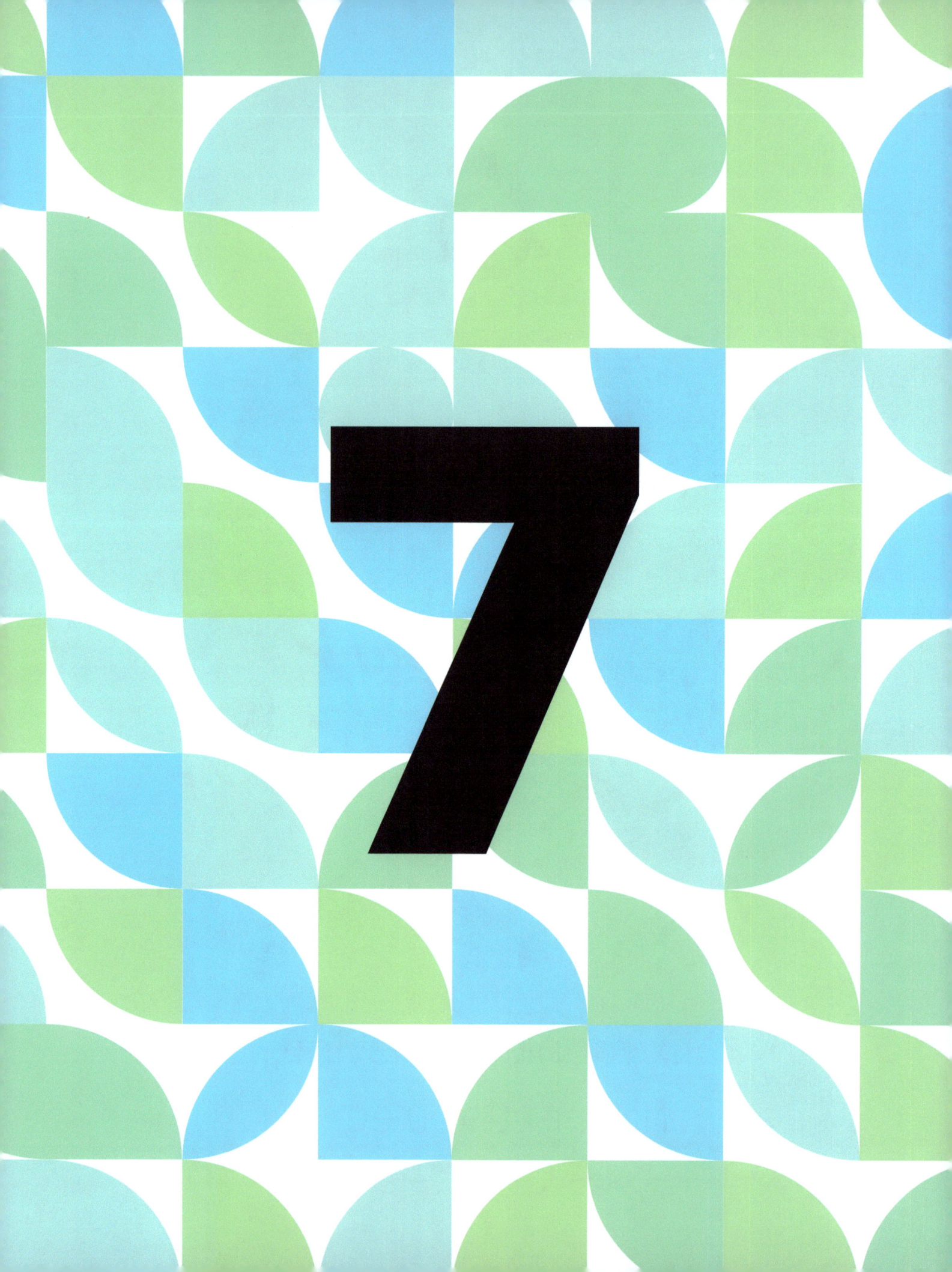

7

Seven little dinosaurs,
all in one truck.

Eight little kittens,
who all got stuck.

9

Nine hungry lions,
let out a big roar.

10

10

Ten happy sharks,
search the ocean floor.

11

Eleven wiggly worms,
all reading a book.

12

Twelve little chicks,
all learning to cook.

13

Thirteen little piglets
are trying on hats.

14

Fourteen small mice are hiding from the cat.

15

15

Fifteen little bunnies are snuggled in bed.

All of the numbers,
they dance in their heads.

Enjoyed this story? Please leave a review on Amazon and help inspire more adventures!

Amazon.com under Kerry E Garner Books

Go to the link, click the book you are reviewing, then hit "Review this Product" at the very, very bottom.

Thank you!

www.ingramcontent.com/pod-product-compliance
Lightning Source LLC
Chambersburg PA
CBHW041538040426
42446CB00002B/149